MW01627573

TRAIN A CHILD IN THE WAY HE SHOULD GO, AND WHEN HE IS OLD HE WILL NOT TURN FROM IT.

PROVERBS 22:6 (NIV)

Special thanks to the illustrator, MRS. SUSAN DRAWBAUGH, who has worked with me for several years, and has given life to the sweet little southern boy in this book.

First Printing, 2018

ISBN: 978-1-63821-824-1

FOR MY BOYS:
anderson william
grady collins
whitten hardy

WHOLESALE CONTACT:
sarahwdudak@yahoo.com

little SOUTHERN GENTLEMAN

to help teach our sons

BY sarah wise dudak
and ILLUSTRATIONS by susan drawbaugh

A *little* southern gentleman is always polite.
He says yes sir, yes ma'am, please, and thank you.

A *little* southern gentleman likes being outside and playing with big trucks, boats, and tractors.

WHD

A *little* southern gentleman
loves home cooked meals,
always drinks his milk,
and cleans his plate.

kDw

A *little* southern gentleman yells
"touchdown"
and roots for his home team.

#1 FAN
HDC
V
EDD

A *little* southern gentleman
brushes his teeth,
combs his hair,
wears gingham,
and puts on cowboy boots.

DWD

A *little* southern gentleman
hugs his daddy
and kisses his mommy.

2020
CALDWELL DRIVE
JMM
+
JMW

A *little* southern gentleman
likes to explore.
He skips rocks and loves to fish.

GLS
HOS

A *little* southern gentleman knows his Bible stories because he is quiet and listens in church.

A *little* southern gentleman is always loyal to his best friend.

JAS

A *little* southern gentleman folds
his hands, bows his head,
and says his prayers every night
before bed.

HPH
JWR

A *little* southern gentleman's favorite colors are red, white, and blue.

WAW

A *little* southern gentleman lets others go first and opens the doors for girls.

JEC

A *little* southern gentleman is a hard worker. He takes good care of his family and house.

GCD
2

The qualities of a

true southern gentleman

are rare and simply special.
He is humble and gentle while
proud and strong.
God, family, and friends
are the center of his life.
He has a happy heart.
He knows exactly
where he comes from.

RJS